inner DEMONS
   outer ANGELS

inner DEMONS outer ANGELS

Joshua 'Porter' Gagnier

Copyright © 2010 by Joshua 'Porter' Gagnier.

Library of Congress Control Number: 2010906673
ISBN: Hardcover   978-1-4500-7837-5
             Softcover   978-1-4500-7836-8
             Ebook   978-1-4500-7838-2

All rights reserved. No part of this book may be reproduced or transmitted in any form or by any means, electronic or mechanical, including photocopying, recording, or by any information storage and retrieval system, without permission in writing from the copyright owner.

This book was printed in the United States of America.

To order additional copies of this book, contact:
Xlibris Corporation
1-888-795-4274
www.Xlibris.com
Orders@Xlibris.com
80067

Contents

Author's Introduction 9
Chapter 1 11

To the Reader 15
Seize the Day...17
Out of control and 19
A friend like you..21
The Devil's Presidential Speech 22
Christ's Rebuttal..23
A Child Growing up 24
A Parent Letting Go 25
A Different take 27
A Dream's Question 29
A Letter to Children..31
A new life..33
Broken Trust 35
Brothers Forever 37
Bygones are Bygones..39
Carbon Copies 41
Enemy to Friend 43
Escape from hell 45
Found At Last 47
Freedom's Ring..49
Champion: Defined 51
Happily Ever After 53
Human Sandpaper 55
I gave in so He could win 57
Insomnia 59
Is this all there is..61
It Starts With Self Doubt 63
Key to Victory...65

What Legacy?	67
Letting It Go	69
Life Lessons	71
Looking Back	73
Mommy? Daddy?	75
My Baby Girl	77
My $C_{17}H_{21}NO_4$	79
My Elysium, where art thou?	81
My Outer Angel	83
My Vicious Love	85
My Why	87
Never Forget	89
No Excuse	91
No Regrets	93
Opposition	95
Passed Due: Payment Required	97
Pray for My Father	99
Praying for Control	101
Q and A	103
Relentless	105
Addiction	107
The Dead Don't Bleed	109
The definition of Hate	111
The Last Two	113
The Never-ending Battle	115
The Riddle	117
Two Years Ago To the Day	119
Uncertainty	121
Which are you: Speaking or being spoken of?	123
WHY	125
Free of 'Friends'	127
Special Thanks	129

Dedicated to Julie, Jeff, and Aaron.

Author's Introduction

It is my opinion life is an infinitely gigantic textured ball bearing. Imagine even a thousandth of a mil shift could change the entire story. It is my belief ever point on this sphere is a different perspective, a different universe. There are more than 6 billion people on this planet—this means there are more than 6 billion universes as well. Granted there is the universe we all live in, but we all have millions of influences both genetic and environmental that make us each different. It is my goal, through my poetry, to move that ball bearing a degree, take a peak into *that* reality, then write my thoughts. If everything is relative, does that not mean the Earth is created about 5 times a second because about 5 people are born every second? On that same thought, does it mean the Earth ends 5 times in that same second because 5 people die during that time?

Not all of my poems are from my perspective. A lot of them are how I interpret actions and reactions of things and people around me. One of my latest poems was 'inspired' by a baseball rolling down a dirt road, so there is no telling 'where I was' when I wrote any particular poem. The purpose of my poetry is to provoke thought—to provoke emotion. I intentionally left every other page blank to allow for writing any thoughts or emotions that may or may not have been provoked while reading these poems.

A lot of people insist they cannot write poetry. Wait, I started in mid thought; people have a misconception poetry has to rhyme—it doesn't. Second, people think poetry has to have rhythm—it doesn't. However, there are a few things, in my opinion, every poem must have. My wife, Julie, insisted she could not "write a poem to save my life", but yesterday wrote one so full of emotion I almost cried. The reason this poem was so awesome? Emotion and thought. I gave her a subject, so to speak. I described a scenario that has never happened but I know is close to her heart. I added the thought, she added the emotion. When she was done she described the experience as *an emotional roller coaster,* and after the first few words, it took on a life of its own.

Join me on this, my emotional roller coaster.

Chapter 1

My Definition of *The Braid*

There are a few of my poems that speak about "a braid". I have included a brief description of what I am referring to.
My physics teacher used Popsicle sticks. First we broke one, then he handed us several. The more sticks there were, the harder it was to break.
A chain is only as strong as its weakest link.
If a chain has 100 cast iron links, and one made from rope, the chain will only hold as long as the rope does.
Both of the above are obvious with physics, though the philosophy can traverse into other realms of life. For example, the mind, body, and soul braid. It seems a person who feels they are weak in one of these three build up the other two. For example, in my experience, those less scholastically inclined worked out a lot. Those who are not physically strong seem to lean heavily on religious beliefs or scholastics in an attempt to strengthen them as a whole. These tendencies are, for the most part, subconscious.
The major misconception is soul=spiritual or religious.
Most forms of martial arts teach a way to strengthen all three simultaneously. The rigorous discipline, the strenuous training, and the long hours of meditation all contribute to strengthening the person as a whole.

The dictionary defines:

Mind: The element, part, substance, or process that reasons, thinks, feels, wills, perceives, judges, etc.

Body: the physical structure and material substance of an animal or plant, living or dead.

Soul: the principle of life, feeling, thought, and actions in humans, regarded as a distinct entity separate from the body and commonly held to be separable in existence from the body.

The combination makes us "who we are". To make them each stronger we must exercise them and let them rest.

Mind: At work all of the time while we are awake. Will not grow or expand through monotonous tasks. These type of tasks tend to drain the mind. Have you ever noticed the last hour of the work day seems to be slow, and you may even feel tired? Have you ever noticed it seems you have more energy 30 minutes after quitting time? This is because of the change in pace, the possibility of new, rather than monotonous, tasks at hand.
To work/relax this part of the braid I would recommend music, audio-books (fiction or non-fiction). Fiction tends to be more relaxing than non-fiction though tastes vary. To relax, take a long bath, or take some time "to stop and smell the roses". Time with family is good, but don't forget to take one on one time with yourself. A lot of people new to the braid concept use this time to plan the next day, this does not constitute relaxing. I don't count watching TV as relaxing because the mind relaxes better with interaction—that is why we dream. Sleep is also important to relax the mind. Oversleeping can make the mind tire; however.

Body: Again, the body is working all day though not always in a positive manner. Working this portion of the braid in a positive manner includes the big cuss work: exercise. Cardio is best and seems to be more thorough. Some weight training is good though overdoing it will put more stress on the body. The phrase "no pain no gain" tends to be exaggerated in this portion of the braid. Exercise in general releases endorphins making us feel better (after the habit is formed). Before the habit is formed, some people get anxious before exercise. Also, strength is built during the resting stage when the body repairs the tears in the muscle. Sleep rests this portion of the braid, but as with the mind, over sleeping can drain the body. Different people require different amounts of sleep. I would recommend starting with the medically recommended hours, then changing it to suit your needs.

Soul: By far the hardest part of the braid to exercise. The soul, in my opinion, is where our conscience, emotion, sense of morality, and self-esteem come from. This part is also the easiest part of the braid to damage. We are bombarded by many definition of physical beauty. If we don't feel we match up (a comparison that should not happen, but does with everyone) that can negatively affect our self-perspective. Break the word down into 'self' and 'esteem'. So that means how well we view ourselves, not how others view us. People in general tend to put more weight on the latter. One way to break this habit is self talk. At first it may feel awkward, that has more to do with how we feel others will perceive our behavior. In the mornings and before bed give yourself a pep talk. In the morning say something like "I will make today great, I will make today better than yesterday. I am a success. I am awesome. I am beautiful." Before bed congratulate yourself on your accomplishments throughout the day. Do not mention setback, slip-ups, or slides.

Express compassion for those you care for. Tell others you love them. Help others when you are able. If you are married, do "chores" your spouse usually does. Make them breakfast in bed. Service is the best and most effective way to strengthen this part of the braid.

One way to relax all three simultaneously is a 2-3 minute relaxation. Every few hours, take 2-3 minutes to breathe, relax, and gather your thoughts; Similar to regrouping for the next assault.

Thoughts

To the Reader

As you read the pages of this book
You will get a glimpse of a look
A look into my heart, mind, and soul
To shed light on my shadow is my goal

We all go through trials and strife
This helps us appreciate the sweeter things in life
There are some dark rhymes
Having been written in darker times

There are others still with a brighter tune
Poetry is my vent—my boon
I don't always know from where they come
They are more than just my sum

I hope as you read beyond this page
You might understand my love, my fear, my rage
We are all more that what meets the eye
We are more than *what* we do—we are *why*

Take a look at the cover art
Of the first poem it is part
The other part is the name
Take a look—they are the same

They are meant to show
No matter what we do—no matter where we go
We cannot defeat our demons alone
We all feel it, but it's not widely known

We need an Outer Angel's aid
I hope through this art, this is portrayed
Alone I never could have won
To *my* Outer Angel: Thank you for all you have done

Thoughts

Seize the Day

If you have never cared
If you have never dared
Dared to feel love's touch
Then you haven't risked that much

If you are too full of yourself to see
Alone is not the way we were meant to be
Then alone you will die—no one will care
All eyes dry—cheeks bare

Quit feeling sorry for yourself and extend a hand
Join the fight to create the Promised Land
Though sometimes you don't believe
You deserve everything you receive

You are loved by the One that matters
With Him on your side adversity shatters
All you need is to ask
Swallowing pride—a daunting task

Ask and ye shall receive
Ask and all of your burdens He will relieve
You must know who you are
And know, that for you, He was spit on, beaten, and scarred

You must grab your life by the reigns
You control your victories and failures; the prize yours to claim
If you want it, you must fight
You must strive for it with all your might

The day is yours, Carpe Diem
You have many allies—you must see them
You must conquer yourself to find
Only you can leave you behind

Thoughts

Out of control and . . .

The exhilaration is almost more than I can take
Everything spinning wildly as my world begins to quake
The feeling of having no control, not in the least
Like being flung around by some gargantuan beast

Yet being so calm and collected makes no sense
Muscles relaxed—mind tense
It feels as though my heart will beat through my chest
Lungs on fire like after a PT test

My muscles ache and I feel weak
Solitude and quiet are all I seek
But without that exhilaration, I feel so alone
Being separated from it hurts worse than a broken bone

There are some readers who already know what I'm talking about
It is one thing, once you know, you can't live without
For this, forever I would pine
I want and need it to always be mine

By now you should have the notion
That I am speaking of an emotion
The 'strongest emotion of them all'
It makes me feel bullet proof and ten foot tall

The best part is not feeling it in you
But to be with someone who you know feels it too
Knowing that both of you are in love and out of control
To know you would together pay any toll

This is dedicated to my one and only love
The one that causes everything above
To the one I love and will every day
Dedicated to my beautiful wife, Julie Gagnier

Thoughts

A friend like you

There is a boy crying somewhere
Crying because nobody cares
He doesn't have any friends
Hopes to have one before life ends

A life of loneliness is no life at all
He is waiting, hoping for the reapers call
Not wishing for death but not wanting to live
For none to this one would attention give

Until one day this boy got the courage to say hi
He didn't even understand why
But he found one—one who would dare
Dare to believe in him—dare to care

Now this boy feels such joy
Like a baby with a brand new toy
He doesn't understand why or how
But to this bond he will always bow

Not understanding the meaning of friend or foe
But this is a friend he does know
Being accepted has never occurred
Of himself he begins to be reassured

One person cared; one person with love in his heart
This pierced his soul—a spiritual dart
He never cared about me or you
Didn't care if we ceased for all he knew

But now he begins to understand
No longer from the public is he banned
He sees the light; sees the sun
Because of the love and friendship of one

Hey Jeff, what's an Eye Dol.
Gotta love this canvesslessness.

The Devil's Presidential Speech

I beseech you to listen to my word
I wish for you to forget others you have heard
Others speak of great death and evil
Stories to prevent ultimate upheaval

Stories of the boogie man
Today we must make stand
We must know that there is no such thing
As an utterly evil being

They want you to grow up in darkness and fear
With the belief that if you disobey you will be burned and seared
The truth is, there is no devil and no hell
Listen to the story that *I* tell

This being of deception is the biggest deceit
It is meant to hold you back—to cause retreat
The possibility of an outside being even caring
The most preposterous, meant to keep you from daring

Daring to push the envelope of society and normality
Trust me this demonic being is only a formality
Science can prove anything with logic and reason
Right down to the changing of every season

So I tell you, unite and come together
Release this world of its useless tether
The confines of rules—of heaven and hell
Listen to the truths *I* tell

There is no devil just as there is no god
There is no rule book; no "iron rod"
Why give power to something or someone that is not there
It is as breathing without air

Christ's Rebuttal

Child we are waiting here for your arrival
My only charge is your soul's survival
I must warn you of a hidden evil,
Of the one who is planning the greatest of upheavals

Trying to hide his true self from site
Hiding behind a false light
The propositions he makes can never come to pass
For he has already lost, our victory will come at last

But fear not my child for I am with thee
No man on earth could even dream of deceiving me
Your family and friends pray every day
That, through the fog, you may find your way

I will gladly be your guiding star
I will carry you until you realize who you truly are
We can never back down from the power of dark
I will protect you from those with The Mark

They dare you to forget
They don't want you to feel remorse or regret
If I could only show you what awaits if you try
If you stand and fight you will never die

You will live with My Father for all eternity
For the rest of time be filled with perfect serenity
I have broken the bonds of death and of hell
I hope you can see the truth in what I tell

When you believe in the Father, in joy you shall bask
And for all eternity this will last
When you do not believe there is a devil
You give him power to increase his evil

A Child Growing up

Sometimes I feel as if I'm being held down
I wish to fly but my wings are bound
What would happen if let go?
Would I be too afraid to grow?

Would I be too used to being grounded
Instead of being well rounded
Would I get lost as soon as I left the nest?
Would I be afraid and wear a mask like the rest

Or would I grow too fast and too bold
Is that the reason for the tight hold?
A death grip, just won't let loose
To afraid to give in, to call a truce

We could work together instead of fight
I could aid in the flight
In turn I could be taught how to live
That is the best gift one could give

Instead of hiding the world from my view
I am smart enough I might learn a thing or too
Maybe you are too afraid I would leave you behind
Do you keep that fear in the front of you mind?

Or do you bury it so no one can see
No one knows what you truly fear is me
You think I might enjoy it too much
You are afraid I will get caught in hell's clutch

The only way to know is to cut the rope
Then all you can do is pray and hope
You have taught me well enough
And brought me up to be tough

A Parent Letting Go

I don't want to see you fail
I would love to see you sail
To soar to great heights and beyond
I just don't want you to break our bond

I am only trying to protect you from the pains of life
I don't want to see you go through strife
If you get lost we will find you
When you have children that is what you would do

I am afraid you gain the wrong friends
And they will bring you to dead ends
I can't let go, you are not ready to be let loose
I love you too much to call a truce

You want to always be right
Instead of allowing me to help in your flight
I was older when I finally learned how to live
I know that is the one gift you want me to give

But I want to keep you safe as long as I am able
I want to make sure you have food on your table
I am afraid you will lose who you are
There's more to life than a fast car

The world is not a nice place
I want to make sure you are ready for the race
If you must go know I love you
No matter what happens this will always be true.

The only way to know is to cut the rope
Then all I can do is pray and hope
I have taught you well enough
And brought you up to be tough

Thoughts

A Different take

Everyone has their own ways to vent
We all have our own schemes
Things we all do when our soul feels bent
This is why the dark themes

I had a lot to get off my chest
But now I have a clean slate
My demons finally at rest
No longer filled with hate

I really never knew love
I never knew what it was like
To be with an angel from above
Like dropping a pack after a twelve mile hike

My guard down—relieved of command
I trust in another, when before I could not
Now together we will stand
For with love, my happiness was bought

From here on out
I see life through new eyes
No longer living in doubt
No longer watching everything die

Seeing things as they live
Leaves me breathless, my tongue paralyzed
But now my happiness I must give
For to keep it is selfish, I realize

I feel free, more than ever before
For now I am loved more than ever
Love feels better than hate when it pierces your core
I say thanks to the man above, only He could be so clever

Thoughts

A Dream's Question

My mind wanders, taking me for a ride
My true thoughts I wish to hide
Hide for eternity for none to see
This world would not let me be me

I want to go when and where I please
Without begging another on my knees
The world doesn't accept my kind
I am the bane in everyone's mind

Everyone has a piece of me inside
In a deep place I reside
Let me out they wouldn't dare
But I like the solitude—so I don't care

I am the king of their thoughts
They are asleep—as programmed robots
Their mind is an amusement park
Though always in the dark

They keep me buried and hidden
To mention me is forbidden
Punishable by death; punishable by life
For life stings worse than death's knife

I would rather die a free soul
Than live fighting for their goal
I am all but I am none
My journey almost complete—almost done

I have been in your conscious mind
I have but one last thing to find
Why do they work so fervently?
When it damns them for eternity

Thoughts

A Letter to Children

Children do not come with an owner's manual
Explaining every detail, every granule
There is not master rule book
Trust me, I have looked

I am sure parents wish there were
Then their hearts wouldn't drop when their child stirs
With this book they would know how to say
"You are the reason I get up every day"

"You are the reason for me"
And they'd say *I love you* where your friends couldn't see
They would know how to express
Why, on good grades, they stress

To them, you deserve nothing but the best
You are their child—they don't care about the rest
Though they may not understand why
When you fuss over a girl or a guy

Their shoulders are always there to drench
Hands always there to pull you out of the trench
They may seem awkward and uncool
But would work three jobs to pay for your school

They would go hungry as long as you are fed
They would sleep on the floor and give you the bed.
So after all is said and done
To their doorstep you should run

You never know when time will cease
And from this life they will be released
Tell them they are the reason for you
Anything they need, you will do

Love you Mom and Dad

Thoughts

A new life

I have a new life I must let the old go
Just leave—they will never know
I wonder if they would even notice me gone
Would they realize life is a great con?

I left them behind and they just let me go
No sadness or regret did they show
They smiled and let me leave their life
This hit my heart like a knife

I didn't get them—they got me
Was I so obvious they could see?
See what was beneath this smile
Could they see my rage so vile?

It doesn't matter if they did or didn't know
Defeat is mine—shame I cannot show
But my revenge is swift—almost complete
I will laugh last—they can't compete

I will a victory of my own
In their pride and supposed glory, Lazy they have grown
Pride goes before a fall—and fall they must
Toward this goal I run—for it I lust

If I win, I also lose
Let it go—or fight—I must choose
If I fight they will know I am shamed
I feel their crosshairs at me aimed

I will give them this victory to save face
They cannot know my disgrace
I have learned from these events
I must let go—this lesson was heaven sent

Thoughts

Broken Trust

Bouncing from house to house—nobody cared
I thought I had found someone who dared
I thought I could tell you anything
You know my life story from the beginning

I thought I knew you—thought I could trust
Of all, I knew you were the most just
I let my guard down because I was home
Come alive no longer a drone

But you shoved me back into the pit
An inner fire has been re-lit
I let it go but you gave it back
Pity and love I again lack

I was coming to the light at the end
Now I realize it was just another bend
This maze of hate, and of doubt
Please someone show me an out

I thought you had lead me the way
But in truth you only lead me astray
All I believe, all I know has been shattered
My pride beaten, broken, and battered

How dare you leave me in this spin?
I wish I didn't know now what I didn't know then
Maybe I could still look you in the eye
Now when I think of you a piece of me dies

My soul is now lost to the abyss
I will always think—"how could you do this?"
They still think you're the best
But believe me—I AM NOT THE REST

Thoughts

Brothers Forever

I miss my brother, I miss my friend
Expect to see you around every bend
We went to war together
There is no describing what we weathered

Then he was shot and killed
His life's blood was spilled
Never to laugh or smile again
I look back on memories every now and then

The stuff we did just being dumb
I just want to cry, but I feel so numb
Why did you leave? Why did you go?
You shouldn't have gone without me in tow

We had so much traveling to do
So much fun to have, me and you
But now you're not here, you've gone away
And I miss you more and more each day

Remember the times in Iraq
The ones you saved me to bring me back
Sorry I could not do the same
Here it's a different game

So many times we should've died
But we came back, glad to be alive
I should have stayed to what you back
But no, there you lie, in a black sack

I am so sorry my friend, my brother
A part of me will forever suffer
One day we will prank angels just to be dumb
I want to cry, but I feel so numb

Aaron Tierno. Friend. Brother. Soldier.

Thoughts

Bygones are Bygones

I am dumped off into someone else's lap
Don't worry I am used to it—I have already snapped
Long ago I went out of my mind
Went searching for one of my kind

Though I didn't find one—I found myself again
I began to care—wondering where I had been
That doesn't matter; I am back now—back to the original me
Now to be what I want to be

Others say I am different—from another plane
I say my life is mine to reign
Some things still bother me—but others just don't
I care about some—but others I just won't

Rule number one: don't sweat the small stuff
Rule number two: anything worth doing is going to be tough
The hardest thing to comprehend
Why did I fear the help of a friend?

I hated being a user
So I fought—no longer a loser
I put myself here so I let myself out
So focused and determined—I can't hear others shout

I wouldn't listen to them even if I could
I don't think anyone should
The trick is, don't care what they say
But you must not become a *they*

Don't shut people out or push them down
A kind king will keep his crown
The ruthless king is feared but will fall
Take a look at history—they get nailed to the wall

Thoughts

Carbon Copies

Where can I go to be alone?
Where can I go so I don't feel cloned?
Too many people are exactly the same
Everyone trying to fit in drives me insane

Why can't people just grow out of it?
When they don't fit in, why throw a fit?
When they don't fit the social norm
They begin to regret the day they were born

Too many people want to be carbon copies
They don't know what they like so they steal another's hobbies
They are too afraid of stepping out of their bounds
So they go to the bar and buy everyone rounds

Too many people try to buy their friends
But once the money's gone the friendship ends
There are too many fakes out there
They're the life of the party, but when alone they just sit and stare

People need to come out of their shell
Instead of falling under another's spell
We want to be somebody other than us
But I don't understand the whole fuss

When I am me, people call me crazy
But in my opinion, y'all are just lazy
Happy just being copies of others
Trying to be like your big brothers

To end this rampage on the copies and clones
I just want to go inside to be alone
At least then I can trust the people there
No longer the life of the party, I just sit and stare

Thoughts

Enemy to Friend

It was futile at best
Fighting constantly without rest
Neither party wanting to give in
Both knowing they are right deep within

Back and forth like childish bickering
People around begin snickering
Pointing and saying "I am glad that's not us"
And my favorite "Like that, we will never fuss"

Others do not understand my adversary
If I give even an inch, I will be buried
Lost and forgotten; never to be heard again
This is why I resist even the slightest bend

I dig deep, pulling out all stops—needing to win
Fighting with a fury that burns deep within
Neither side wanting to call a truce
Both aiding in tying the noose

Both willing to face death before defeat
Pushing forward, never calling retreat
Both reminding the other of past events
In an effort to cause their enemy to relent

Words cutting deeper than a blade
Both feeling utterly betrayed
I draw back to throw the first blow
No remorse do my eyes show

Thrusting forward my fist clenched tight
Into this hit, I focus all my might
A loud crash as I shatter the mirror
After defeating myself, my path becomes clearer

Thoughts

Escape from hell

The world swirls around in a blinding blur
I run from nightmares my dreams conjure
They nip and growl but never touch
I can never leave—they have weakened me too much

They don't touch my body but they tear at my soul
I guess my insanity is their goal
Though I feigned insanity for my own cause
Maybe they would let me out—for this I give myself applause

For deceiving the masters of deception and despair
Like winning a hand of poker without so much as a pair
They have checked—giving me the lead
The warnings—they would never heed

Now on the offense I beat them down
Their crying and screaming such a joyous sound
I am winning—conquering all who put me here
At my triumph—they start to sneer

Though I have won this battle—can I win the war?
I have come close to winning in the past—but could never open the door
The door that keeps me in the dark
This key draws me like blood does a shark

I am drawn to it but it always eludes me
What is out there, I can't wait to see
The key has been found the door is unlocked
Now they will be left down here—their exit blocked

But I just left one cell for a new one
I calculate my next move—I know what must be done
With the power to destroy this jail
I have the power to destroy my inner hell

Thoughts

Found At Last

For many years I have toyed with the thought
Of finding the one I forever sought
What would I say, how would I act?
Would I approach the situation with the right tact?

All this pondering and thinking leaves me wanting
The thought that she is out there so very taunting
I search high; I search low, and everything in between
I start to give up, toward defeat, I lean

But I hate quitting so I pick up my pace,
As if sprinting the last straightaway of the race
The goal is within my reach
I wonder of the things she could teach

I found someone who knows somebody
Though the waters seem a little muddy
I don't know if this information I can trust
I don't care; I am consumed with the lust

The lust of the victor's crown
Sure enough, I wasn't let down
I now know where the one could be found
I feel as if I am homeward bound

With this victory came even more hearsay
I was the youngest child, until today
I found my mother who I had longed to hug and kiss
And I found a sister whom I had missed

I started with a name
And with that piece, I have won the game
I finally found the one I sought
My quest ended better than I thought

Thoughts

Freedom's Ring

We all have our skeletons in our mind's dark recess
It seems we bear these secrets on our heart's crest
We keep them hidden from everyone around
But in our memory they resound

And every now and then someone will say
Something that will take us right back to that day
The day we wish we could go back and change
The one moment we feel makes us the most deranged

In our minds we imagine what life would be like
If we could just remove the searing spike
Remove it from the bleeding wound in our thoughts
But no matter how much we try, it is all for naught

We grit our teeth against the pain
Trying to forgive ourselves in vain
No matter how at ease we feel
The remorse and throbbing is always fresh and real

The memory is like that theme park souvenir
When you're not looking for it, its ugly head will rear
It will always find you no matter how you bury it
It can always climb out no matter how deep your mind's pit

So I say let it out, let it be free
Once in the open you will see
There is always someone who can help relieve the strain
Share the load with one you trust and release the pain

The one who helped me the most has no clue
Maybe one day I could show how much I value
To the one who helped me praises I sing
To the one who helped me . . . I gave a wedding ring

Thoughts

Champion: Defined

Not as often as it should be
A person sees a champion and says: That will be me
Not it *could* be but that it has already come to pass
They look at the future instead of the past

Champions don't wait for doors to open
Don't spend time waiting and hoping
Hoping that something good will land in their lap
Their goals in line, drawn like a map

They build on what they know and go from there
Being the few who dare
To push themselves so hard they want to cry
Push to the point they feel as if they are going to die

A champion knows they can't stand still
They are either falling or fighting up the next hill
Even if beaten they cannot be defeated
They know with other giants of time they will be seated

There is no retreat, no surrender, and no backing down
Getting back up every time their face meets the ground
The fear of failure is drastically outweighed by the need
A need so thick they can feel it, the need to succeed

A champion has a stronger spirit and fewer broken bones
Because they learn from what other champions have shown
I cannot lose is not the same as *I will win*
Only you will know which burns within

Champions are not always Olympians or sports stars
A true champion helps you find who YOU really are
They are the ones willing to help—to show you the way
The ones who will back you up both night and day

Thank you Tony and Alice.

Thoughts

Happily Ever After

If I had one wish, it would be for one day
One day to *show* you instead of *say*
How much you mean to me
How without you I would not be

I dare not mutter the words "I love you"
Because these words just wouldn't do
For the right words don't exist nor will they ever
So to describe my love to you is my greatest endeavor

Though you say you are the lucky one
I ask my lucky star, what I must have done
To win your heart and earn your hand
When you said yes, I arrived at my promised land

I will bask in your light
And hold you with all my might
You are the one I prayed for
You light up a room when you enter the door

In truth I think this sounds rather cliché
But with you all week I want to lay
Is cliché really such a bad thing
Happily ever after is all clichés bring

I want to live happily ever after
And fall asleep to your sweet laughter
And make you cry tears of joy
When we have a baby girl or boy

I look forward to hugging you;
To walking barefoot through morning dew.
I look forward to living in the grace of the Master
Here's to living happily ever after.

Thoughts

Human Sandpaper

People say I am mean and abrasive
And ask how, with myself, can I live
I promise I will not lose any sleep
But maybe I could give just a peek

A glimpse of how I think
But it may bring you to the brink
Right up to your wits end
Don't try to change it, I will not bend

I am definitely not what people see
I never let anyone see the real me
Don't let them see my inner boiler
That would be a movie spoiler

Everyone does it whether or not they admit
Inside their head is a deep viper's pit
Everyone is a snake when they have to be
But being one when it's not needed is my key

I am always searching for the next rung on the ladder
Using everyone possible—it doesn't matter
Yet to meet an opponent I couldn't be beat
Yet to taste the bottom of another's cleat

Everything happens for a reason, they say
My reason is to be better off at the end of the day
Every day is a war to stay afloat—to stay ahead
To lead the pack instead of being lead

Not following someone else's reasons why
Their rules of where I will go when I die
I know where I'm headed at the end of my existence
I deserve it after all of my persistence

Thoughts

I gave in so He could win

Sometimes I feel I am outside looking in
Looking in on my own life from a window within
I see what I am doing but cannot change
Watching myself become deranged

In a corner of my mind—not in control
I want my life back I will pay the toll
No matter the cost I want to be free
Free from whatever has this control over me

I have a life but I feel like a zombie
Locked in a room outside of my own body
Why do I lock me up—for what goal?
As long as I rule I will never be whole

I want to get on with my life
I want to be loved—by one willing to help me through strife
Love and hate seem to blend here
But the hurt from hate more deeply sears

Sears my body from the inside out
I must survive my next spiritual bout
For if I gain enough strength He will rule
I will no longer be my demon's tool

I want to live I want to love
I have found an angel sent from above
I can't say how I feel as long as I am a slave
I must let Him win—send my pride to its grave

I can see victory now—He has almost won
The fight is coming close to being done
He is the victor, love is my prize
I am now free from my illusions—free from my lies

Thoughts

Insomnia

I can't sleep at night because of the monster in my head
Not from closet or under the bed
This beast resides inside
During the day in the shadows it hides

But when the stars come out in the night
I close my eyes; it's in my sights
In the beginning the battles were easily won
The war rages on—never really done

Days begin to blur as the battle rages within
I cannot tell where I end and my devil begins
The mirror no longer reflects *me*
It shows only what I let others see

I can't tell the difference anymore
It burns the mind to the very core
Bushes come alive and shadows talk
Somewhere between real and sleep is where I walk

Never truly asleep, never truly awake
I am grateful for my nightmare's sake
At least I don't see them screaming
But being awake, life is no longer beaming

Life is like a black and white television
Static buzzing in my head like a deep incision
Body and mind overtaxed
Always on edge, never relaxed

Awake—how many days?
Face pale—eyes circled and glazed.
The beast takes control of my head
I guess I will sleep when I am dead

Thoughts

Is this all there is

Running laps every week of every year
Off this track I dare not steer
My life is laid before me I dare not change
The path chosen for me—I dare not rearrange

Though I cannot see the end of my years
I still try to push through with minimal tears
The finish line must be on approach
I don't know if I can take another reproach

Another dose of life—a dose of this monotonous existence
Hunting for my freedom with such persistence
I am now the hunter, no longer the prey
I am the leader, no longer just part of the fray

But I have been here before
But I could never quite reach the door
The door that leads out
I keep going—no time to stand about

Now I am once again the hunted
My apparent progress shunted
Never going where I haven't already been
Just beyond my reach must be Zen

I need rest, I need peace and quiet
I can't stand being in constant riot
Okay, the door is now closer than ever
Today may be the end of my endeavor

I swing open the door in utter shock
I hear laughter as my body begins to rock
Another track to run—another corporate ladder
I keep running my spirit beaten and battered

Thoughts

It Starts With Self Doubt

All my life I built these walls
To protect myself against life's squalls
I am the stray dog I don't want
The limp cat that I taunt

It just adds to the great barriers
I'm not the disease—only a carrier
Locked within I can't let me out
My voice raspy—I can no longer shout

The walls are closing in
Suffocating me from within
I try to climb out—try to see the light
But I kick myself down—so I give up the fight

I can't tell but inside I'm dying
I laugh out loud though inside I'm crying
This hate and fear caused a void inside
Demons enter my soul—here the devil resides

I hear snickering and laughter when nobody is there
Open my eyes—I would not dare
I don't do anything anymore
I just sit and stare at the locked door

I have no choice but to stay
Locked within—is it night or day?
I don't want to eat—I cannot sleep
I want to but I am buried to deep

I lay down to let my soul go
Dead or alive—I really don't know
Do I care if I am living or breathing?
I don't think so—why else am I leaving

Thoughts

Key to Victory

To be afraid is not less than man
To run instead of making a stand
Everyone has fear inside their hearts
Hate, love, fear, and courage in a balanced art

Some gravitate toward fear because of their life
Most people never fall in love for fear of strife
Love is to hurt, some might think
Though it brings you to heaven's brink

Without love in my day
I would never have had the courage to find my way
Though I am not totally home, I am coming close
Though I feel like a devil sometimes, I am loved by a heavenly host

At one point in your life or another
Your fear will hide what needs to be discovered
Even great generals of war
Have fear pounding on their heart's door

But the feeling of victory is greater than loss
Some want to feel it at all costs
They want it so bad they trample others
And wouldn't look back, given their druthers

Too busy to notice those they stepped on
Trying to go it alone, instead of building the bond
The comradery of the team
Should leave you bursting at the seams

Winning alone leaves you alone and so much colder
Winning with the weak is oh so much bolder
Lifting the weak so they may see
When it comes to victory—Love is the Key

Thoughts

What Legacy?

Where in the universe do I fit?
I ponder this while at my desk I sit
I have yet to find my place in time
A place in the history books I call mine

I have yet to find myself
The antique book forever on the shelf
No one dares to pull me down from my place of rest
I keep telling myself it is for the best

Though I am having trouble believing
That my life will be a legacy upon my leaving
But I have a long path yet to travel
My life has more twine yet to unravel

Time travels faster the more it unwinds
Hopefully before it is empty my place I will find
My mark on history my 'ode to Glory'
To have bards of our day tell my story

My song isn't a proud one thus far
Less of a melody—more of a scar
My entire life I have been tracking
Trying to find that which is lacking

When will I rise triumphant?
A hero returning to the sound of trumpets
In one hundred years will people remember me?
I would hate to be around in that day to see

To see my reputation forever shrouded in mystery
Instead of standing the test of history
This is my life's only goal and quest
I wish to be legendary—to become the best.

Thoughts

Letting It Go

Far from humanity
In the middle of nowhere inches from insanity
On the verge of doing nothing at all
My mind is elsewhere—thoughts in a tight ball

I can't feel the pain anymore
I am pain and anguish's whore
Where is my nirvana, where is my peace?
Instead I am stuck—my life on lease

I go where I have never dreamed of going
I have knowledge I never dreamed of knowing
Here to do someone else's dirty work
Deep within my being I toss and jerk

Hold it in—a voice says, so calm so pure
Is this my conscience or my eternal lure?
Can't let it out—not mine to give
Without my soul's prison—could I live?

I am going to live forever in their thoughts
Those who put me here, their minds now in knots
I am in control now, finally at peace
I own this prison—no longer on lease

This prison is my castle, my love
My prison has become my velvet glove
I am here but there
I am in the middle of everywhere

I control my space I control my time
The world controls me no more—my life is now mine
I am free inside—soon to be free for real
Finally have time for my wounds to heal

Thoughts

Life Lessons

I am blind to the big scheme
I still ask myself: what does it all mean
Jumping from here to there and beyond
Always trying to find where I belong

Never sure, never knowing where I am going
Though through this confusion my mind has been growing
There is a reason for everything—I read that somewhere
Why this, why me—can I ask, do I dare?

Looking back, all seems so planned, so precise
Like a game of chess, or a maze made for mice
So many turns—so many roads
The destination always the same—this I know

Lessons taught and lessons learned are lessons none the less
If we don't have to learn the hard way—we are counted blessed
Either way we learn the same
Still find the end to the maze—finish the game

Some take wrong turns, or so we think
Though their choices and turns are linked
You go straight but they turn
For their lesson—they got burned

You both cross the finish line of death
You both pass on—when you breathe your last breath
It is easier to learn from another's mistakes
But then you wouldn't know if you have what it takes.

Have you really lived if you only watched?
You didn't leave a mark—leave your notch
Go play—go have fun—just keep in mind
This poem as your time unwinds

Thoughts

Looking Back

Words cannot express, but I will try
Everything I do feels like I am about to die
But that still doesn't express
How I always worry—never at rest

Almost like the Devil in my head
Faking smiles, thought inside I am dead
I want to let it out, but I am afraid
In my grave, I'd rather be laid

I do not expect you to understand
Like a language of a foreign land
I wouldn't have enough tears
Even If I cried for thousands of years

Can someone please dive into my hell?
Then *maybe* you'd understand the story I tell
Be warned you *will* be torn apart
A constant thorn through the heart

Out of my prison I want to be lead
Then, maybe, I'll want to get out of my bed
I beg and plead to be let out
But it seems I ignore my shouts

I cry because no one can see
That I have become my worst enemy
Don't leave me here
Your company is all I hold dear

We are to the end of my tale
I only wish I had the wind in my sails
Then I'd go with you when you leave
Then myself I wouldn't deceive.

Thoughts

Mommy? Daddy?

My insides begin to boil with pain and hate
Hate of love that comes too late
Anger begins to overwhelm my soul
This animosity has taken its toll

Too many people roam this earth
Without knowing the reason for their birth
Too many parents don't love their seed
Too many children sit at home as their hearts bleed

Bleeding with the need of attention—the need of love
Feeling forsaken by even God above
All it takes is to know they are cared for
Instead of sending them to a room behind a locked door

Are the words "I love you" too hard to even whisper
Your daughter, when was the last time you kissed her
When was the last time you took just one minute out of your day?
To tell her that for her safety and happiness you pray

It is Mommy's and Daddy's job to kill the boogeyman
Not to become their child's nightmares damned
When was the last time you showed concern?
Instead of always scolding—always stern

Do you know how they feel?
Do you care if they will eat their next meal?
Too many mommies and daddies become their child's blight
Instead of helping them through life's plight

You must hold them close to your heart
Love should not be forced, it is a beautiful art
You must know it to give it
If you do not love yourself . . . you cannot share it

If you think this is about you. It is.

Thoughts

My Baby Girl

I met you today, and I'm in love
My little Athena from above
You look so much like your mother
I will love you like no other

Your mom couldn't be here today
God called her home; she couldn't stay
You have her eyes—you have her nose
You were born with ten fingers—ten toes

Healthy and strong
In my arms is where you belong
I want to hold you for eternity
Forever wrapped in sweet serenity

But that can't come to pass
For childhood is not meant to last
I hope as you grow,
Care and love is all I show

There will come a time we don't see eye to eye
I hate seeing you hurt, I hate seeing you cry
I pray your mother is watching over you
For I cannot see everything you do

I want to keep you safe from harm
I don't want you taken in by his charm
I know you are grown, but I still care
To anyone who wishes you harm, beware

I look at you as I walk you down the aisle
Through my tears I can see you smile
You will always be my baby girl.
I only wish I could give you the world.

Thoughts

My $C_{17}H_{21}NO_4$

Around you I feel that I can come out of my shell
With you, I feel safe from even the deepest of hells
When you enter a room I am drawn to you by strong impetus
Sometimes I cannot tell if this is love or lust

You and I are as natural as sugar and water's epitaxy
When you are near I am filled with such ecstasy
You are my foundation, my substrate
When I see you my heart beats at an elevated rate

Even when we are mere angstroms apart
I can feel the longing of my heart
When we are apart nothings seems copasetic
When you're gone it rains a rain that they could never predict

When you're not around everyone feels berated
Because every moment you're gone is excruciatingly hated
I cannot hold it back even with the strongest of wills
Every moment your gone I long for the chills

The chills that creep up and down my spine
When I hold you close for I know you are mine
When, from each other, we are separated
Life itself seems dilapidated

You are the greatest of any dependency
The need to be with you is my only tendency
Some people need what is in the title, I need you more
When you are around you make me soar

The reason big or uncommon words were used
Is to leave you bewildered and confused
You turn me upside down and all around
When I am with you to reality I am no longer bound

Thoughts

My Elysium, where art thou?

There is nothing as far as the eye can see
How did this desolation come to be?
Hearing what isn't there
Howling voices are everywhere

This place cursed to eternal damnation
Hated from the dawn of creation
Minions and devils make this place home
Exiled to this hole—into hell thrown

Burning angry during the day
Flames licking our soul as we pray
We pray for security to be safe through the night
We hope there is a god to aid us in this fight

This fight against our own thoughts
Our morals and beliefs tied in knots
That is why we are in this baring straight
We are preparing to enter hell's gate

We became what we have cursed
Into flames of cold and fear we burst
We become one with the void that we have shunned
We now pay for deeds we've done

Some will pay for what they didn't do
I will pay and so will you
We are all minions here you see
Some just don't admit to what they are afraid to be

I am nothing as far as the eye can see
I am desolation cause by insanity
I am voices that aren't there
Feeding off pain I am everywhere

Thoughts

My Outer Angel

When I first met you I thought I must be dead
Don't make assumptions until all is read
I thought I had left my life behind
I thought my certificate of death had been signed

I was floating as if I had passed on
All of the problems of life were gone
No longer did I have to work and toil
No longer did hate in my veins boil

It was a peaceful experience
The thought that I had left existence
I was finally free from flesh and its weakness
No longer drowning in bleakness

I could go anywhere and do anything I wanted
By the demons I was no longer haunted
I could fly to the moon and back
Worries of the world I did lack

I felt as if I had gone out into a sunny day
My eyes not quite adjusted to the sun's rays
I thought I had given up the ghost
And I was now in the presence of heavenly hosts

From that moment on all I wanted to do was please
Life began to come with ease
I felt drunk though sober as the day I was born
Life's blanket came together, no longer torn

That day I had found something so precious and pure
I had found the one who could help me endure
My life was no longer mangled
Because in you I found my Outer Angel

Thoughts

My Vicious Love

The world, as I know it, has ended
My life is not what I intended
I am alone within my prison
Removed from the only home I ever lived in

My love has left, my life has gone
Tell me what went wrong
I have sold everything I hold dear
Please, do not come near

I must punish myself for what I have done
I cover all of the windows to hide the sun
The room is dark now so no one can see
What I have become, what I led myself to be

I reach into my bag and pull out my love
Pricking my veins it lets me float to heaven above
Lets me float above life—above pain
This is the only thing that keeps me sane

I feel the warmth start in my arm and begin to consume
No longer do the memories loom
Free from pain and from strife
Now free from even life

I must enjoy this flight
For it no longer lasts through the night
Needing more of my love and more often
I need more to lift me from my coffin

I am beginning to fall faster than before
Careening back to reality—toward the floor
I shake uncontrollably; I am forced out of heaven above
Once again, I reach into my bag and pull out my love

Thoughts

My Why

Every person living today
Has a set of rules they obey
Reasons to do what they believe is right
Different motivations to fight the good fight

Some people use respect of humanity
Others do it to keep their sanity
There are people who use common sense
Others still, fight to make life less tense

Some have a fear of their God
Others have reasons we might find odd
Some do what is right as a personal crusade
Others get a personal high from coming to another's aid

Men do it to impress women
Women to impress men
All these reasons are well and good
Whatever keeps people doing what they believe they should

Though we have yet to explain my reason why
Mine is a fear of where I go when I die
But not so much a fear of hell
Or even fear of a jail cell

My reason comes from much deeper
Believe you me, it is not the Grim Reaper
For death has no power to make me quake
I do what is right for my love's sake

For I have joined with one from above
An angel that I so dearly love
And when she is called to return home
I want to go with her; not alone

Thoughts

Never Forget

Love is a great weapon for life
Hate is the same—but that of strife
One cannot love and hate simultaneously
Though some hide hate behind a smile so heinously

I wish love from all views was the same
I wish love was not thought a game
Hate seems to rule more often than not
Everyone's anger and fear burns too hot

Too hot to feel the chill up their spine
Like the one I felt when I met this love of mine
I want all to feel what I do inside
This warmth of love doesn't burn or hide

Hate has too many faces too many fronts
If you can't recognize love you must hunt
What is the point of the chase?
Time spent hating is all a waste

Why can't we all just get along—has been said
Said so often the true meaning is obviously dead
I wish we could love all mankind
Hating all is like a death warrant we have signed

But too many people sign their own death warrant
They didn't even see the miracle no matter how many heaven sent
Hate is not of heaven, love is not of hell
Love is freedom—hate is a prison cell

The moral of this rhyme should be clear
Let every man hear
That one man loved all—our eldest brother
The same who said "Let us love one another"

Thoughts

No Excuse

People don't understand you
They question everything you do
They push, they point, and they laugh
Making you feel less than half

You bottle it and keep it
Adding fuel to your fire pit
One day they will understand
Then they wouldn't dare raise their hand

One day you will pay them back
Their jokes, humor will lack
One day laughing will stop
The carnage, they will have to mop

But no matter how much they taunt
You know your actions in your mind will haunt
No matter how much they poke fun
There is no excuse for what you've done

You couldn't live with your actions
So you removed their satisfaction
Thinking of what you did you just sit and pout
Heavy with guilt you took the coward's rout

To many lives on that day were extinguished
Your own humanity you chose to relinquish
If you wanted to die that could have been arranged
But to take the life of another first is blatantly deranged

Now I hope you enjoy the kiss of the flames
Just remember you have only yourself to blame
I hope you don't rest for an eternity
And to those who were lost, I hope you find serenity

Dedicated to those lost December 1, 1997; April 20, 1999; April 16, 2007.
This is dedicated to all lives lost in all massacres through time.

Thoughts

No Regrets

In school the teachers would ask
What you wanted to be if getting money was an easy task?
If you had all the money you would ever need
In what profession would you choose to succeed?

The purpose behind this query
Is to show what you want to be, clearly
In essence it would work if done right
If you keep your goals in your sight

Now that I have reminded you of this
What would you miss?
If you had a short time left to exist
What one thing would you be unable to resist?

Just as important if not more so
What would you regret if you had to go?
Would you want to change anything?
What attitude would you bring?

If any of these questions made you reminisce
It would be a good suggestion to go get what you would miss
Go do what you would regret not doing and fast
Because believe you me forever, life does not last

We are on this planet for such a small stretch
Only a few of us get the big catch
The reason for this is instead of confidence and self clout
We have self pity and self doubt

You don't want to wish 'you could have done'
Don't want to wish what you could have won
Always look toward the stars—never look down
Only then will victory resound

Thoughts

Opposition

I am the furthest point away
Yet I am closer than death's decay
I am inside your mind yet outside thought
I am within your core—though, you, I am not

I am all things, yet none
Master of the past, present and future—look what's been done
You can't get rid of me you cannot hide
Within is where I reside

Try to push me aside and you will die
For without me you wouldn't know peace—that is no lie
You must appreciate what you have
You must have a wound to appreciate the salve

Without death there is no life
Without happiness there is no strife
You must be sick to be well
You must know heaven to know hell

Opposites are true in all things
Resonating through your entire being
There is no sanity without insanity
No destruction and pain—without humanity

If you never live you—you will be immortal
If you never die—you are not of this portal
To die is to be born—to be born is to die
To know the truth you must know the lie

To sleep you must wake
To give you must take
Without health there is no disease
Without struggle—there is no ease

Thoughts

Passed Due: Payment Required

My voice enters your mind, audible venom
You try to lock me out but I find your mind's plenum
Through back doors you try to brick and wall
But you still answer when I call

You are unknowing soldiers who, in death, will serve
You will fight for the evil we will strive to preserve
All will be targets, rich and poor alike
None will know when this army will strike

They damn themselves with their words
They come to me in droves and herds
All wanting power without a price
To my spider's web they are enticed

But they are unaware of the penalties within
The penalties of their gravest sins
In walk men and out walk devils
In their new glory they revel

They forget the small print of the contract
In their fortune they become lazy and relaxed
Unaware of the piper that waits to be paid
Unwilling to accept the destiny which they have laid

They come kicking, screaming and all alone
But they are bound to become my drones
To uphold their end of the bargain
To fulfill their contract to the very end

Now my attention turns to you, the reader
Will you just follow me, or be the leader
What venom have you let escape your vocal chords
Will your fight me, or join my hordes?

Thoughts

Pray for My Father

I grew under your wing
I wanted to be like you in everything
You were the master of all
Never did I imagine you could fall

Fall so low—even through the bottom
I know what you're thinking—I got 'em
Yeah ya did—you even got me
You were too good—too perfect—no one could see

But I now know there are demons within
Your embrace engulfs me with sin
All think you to be a king
Everyone, your praises sing

I saw through the primer covering the rust
I saw deep beneath the crust
I saw a glimpse behind the mask
Believe me I did not want the task

It hurts too much to believe
All my life, you had me deceived
I looked up to you
You are my *father*—I'm supposed to

But now I can't even fathom
How beneath the smile was such a phantom
Lurking in the darkness like a beast
All are your prey, on their trust you feast

But you don't prey on me now
I may never forget, but I will forgive—somehow
My wounds will heal; I will be whole
I pray to God to care for your soul

Dedicated to children who were not loved the way they should have been.
To my father, thank you for never becoming what is described here.

Thoughts

Praying for Control

On this page it is written
Of pain, hate, and the love smitten
The forgotten story—never spoken
Vengeful lust of the heart . . .—broken

Maybe one day you'll read this and feel
This fear so deep, so pure, so real
Maybe you will understand what I know
And understand the great length I go

I must go the extra mile to keep from cracking
But every day you have those who are backing
Backing the weak into a corner—further and deeper
One day I will be their grim reaper

One day I will lose the only thing holding me
Maybe then they will see
Nobody would see it coming before it strikes
Or see the wolf before it bites

If she was ever taken from my life
I would take revenge on those who cause only strife
Cut them straight to the bone
Onto the wicked and evil vengeance would be honed

They would never feel safe
I would be their eternal wraith
They would pray to the God they denied for so long
And be terrified of doing the littlest thing wrong

So every day I kneel and pray
That I would die before that day
Before I lose control of my inner devils
And bring hell on earth to a new level

Thoughts

Q and A

One day a man asked me a question:
"If she were ever taken, what would be the lesson?"
I quickly and sternly responded to his query with care
I would let my demon from its lair

For the only things keeping me sane
Her smile, her love, like a bathing rain
If my tether were ever cut
The world would cry indoors with windows shut

Every criminal, every rapist, every thief
Would face an executioner beyond belief
Rage and fury would flow free
And I hope I die before that day I see

Because in my wake would be such decay
A decay of evil in the world today
Vengeance would be mine and mine alone
The underworld would quake to the bone

For the vigilantes in comic books
Don't show how it really looks
Nobody would even care
They would carry on without despair

Child rapists would be at the top of my list
Then to killers, I think you get the gist
The law wouldn't be enough pain
To keep the drug dealers blood from falling like rain

The man quickly left me alone
I guess my words chilled him to the bone
I forgot to tell him one last thing
About the safety and security to the innocent I would bring

Thoughts

Relentless

"Take the road less travelled" they say
But they don't mention the price you'll pay
Blazing a new path has its toll
Both on the body and the soul

You must first decide
Where in history you wish to reside
Are you willing to be scarred and beaten?
Willing to be scoffed at as a cretin?

Are you willing to take a seat where you are not allowed?
Can you proclaim your dream in front of a crowd?
Your final goal must be worth everything
It must fill every fiber of your being

Going in half hearted would be the greatest blunder
Go all in or you will be torn asunder
If you quit, nothing will be gained.
Only you will be left to blame

You must view it as required,
Instead of simply desired.
Act as though it has already occurred
Never let your vision become blurred

Create the future you deserve,
Don't merely sit back and observe
The world is ours; it is what we make it
It will not be given, you must take it

Decide how much it means to you
Then decide what you will do
Decide the difference you want to make
Then decide which road to take.

Thoughts

Addiction

Closing all around so tight I cannot breathe
This pain and hate—I must relieve
I know not how but I must find out
It won't let me go no matter how I shout

It comes back more often now, and I am getting weak
I shut myself in, but through the floor it sneaks
My armor rusted, my sword dull from the fight
I cannot win, not with all my might

I am the bullied child
My feelings running wild
I wish I could just fall into a dark hole
Why does it still torment my soul?

For every year I gain—it gains ten
The only thing between me and Zen
Too tired to fight anymore
I don't care, so I open the door

Let it in, let it feast
It leaves sooner now at least
Though it grows hungry more often
My soul is dead—my body—a coffin

I feel everything close around me
Why won't it just leave me alone—leave me be
Pain is pain no matter what kind
But pain of the body beats pain of the mind

It has subsided for now—for how long
I can hear its war chant—its battle song
It is coming back again
When will I be free? WHEN?!!

Thoughts

The Dead Don't Bleed

Alone I sit and I ponder
I let my thoughts flow, my mind wander
Then my thoughts rest on those things
The one's I hide from other beings

So I begin to punish myself with a blade
For all of the mistakes I have made
Cutting deep enough for maximum pain
It calms the guilt, make me feel sane

Just a bit of a reminder that I am living
This reminder gives me such thanksgiving
The warmth trickles down my arm and drips to the floor
Such is the release; wanting for more

I don't want to die
So I guess that leaves them asking why
Why I willingly do this to myself, and often
If I do not want to be laying in my own coffin

Why do people do oh so many things they do
If you have seen what I have seen, you might do it too
I will try to explain the best I can
Explain why I cause as much pain I can stand

Imagine all of your pain dripping
All of your hate from you slipping
That is my hate there in that puddle
You cope; your ways a little more subtle

Seeing myself cut and flowing
Keeps my hurt from growing
I guess I do it for a need
A need to know I'm alive, because the dead don't bleed.

Thoughts

The definition of Hate

I kill all sorrow, and signs of remorse
I cause even the devil to be coarse
For he will never reach my level of evil
My true power—I must never reveal

My heart is black as nothingness, dark as night
My soul is the plague you all fight
I am pestilence I am desolation
I am the end of all creation

I feed off fear—hate is my name
Killing hope is a sport—a child's game
My robes tainted black
I temp suicide—use the gun on the rack

I hate all around me—a demon I may be
Laughing loudly for they don't know—or choose not to see
Hold my hand as I lead the way
Your life—an instrument I play

I am the puppeteer; I am your master
Because of me you burn faster
Causing paranoia—driving you insane
As you kill each other—power I gain

What I have learned cannot be taught
I received the power have I sought
Living with the devil has its perks
Laughing when you fall—in the shadows I lurk

Armageddon is my goal
I will burn all of your souls
To gain true power I would kill
Now because of my power you die still

Thoughts

The Last Two

One day the world will know
The hell in which I live, the fire in which I grow
This hate consumes me inside and out
Believe you me it is not just clout

The seven deadly sins would look like a child's game
If my sins were ever to be claimed
For vanity, greed, and envy
Would have no burden over me

And to the sloth and gluttony I would say
Which is worse your way or my way?
Trust me I would choose the latter
For the definitions of evil I would shatter

If you have an eye so keen
You will learn what I mean
If you pay attention you would see
I left out the last two, what could they be

The last two mean absolutely nothing if you read
My words you know you must heed
I take the place of the last two deadly sins
When you scream, it will be a silent din

Now I only take up the last two
One day I will show it to you
My plan to rid the world of evil
Is the world ready for such an upheaval?

In my eternal lust for power
You will see me in you last hour
Now my wrath will be released
And trust me it will never cease

Thoughts

The Never-ending Battle

Tossing, turning—trying to sleep
Into every pore they seep
Haunting cries of the past
They creep in when I lower my mask

The façade of peace that I show friends
The one I lower when the day ends
I hide my inner fiend, lock it in tight
It always finds a way out when not in sight

Every waking moment is a nightmare
All I see is the open eyed death stare
Not seeing anything but seeing it all
All those things I wish I couldn't recall

Death of the past never leaves
Through my keep's walls it easily cleaves
Piercing through to my very core
Twisting the blade of guilt once more

Burning deep with agonizing torment
I must begin my path toward enlightenment
For I took great pleasure in their defeat
The fact that I would've done anything to see them beat

Peace will come in due course
Until then, I am swallowed by remorse
I stare back at those wide eyes of death
Grit against the pain—holding my breath

I breathe deeply entering sweet slumber
Once again I don't feel encumbered
Peace from the day's battle has come once again
As I sleep, in my dreams I arrive at Zen

Thoughts

The Riddle

You cannot see where I end and you begin
While I am around you will never win
Holding you back, holding you down
You cannot fly—I keep you bound

You need me like your next breath
Though I may cause your death
You only like how I make you feel
Away from reality I let you peel

One day you will see
You are nothing because of me
Your very soul is mine
Control you chose to resign

My clutches cannot be escaped
Every recess of your braid I have raped
I am the reason you have no friends
The reason you always hit dead ends

Even if left behind
I will always be there in the back of your mind
For my touch you will always crave
Let me guide you to your grave

Have you ever asked how you got here?
Why your life is not yours to steer?
When you picked me up, you knew me
You knew, but chose not to see

You will forever ask yourself why,
Why did you even start, why did you even try?
I am the poison you add to your veins
Now it is I, not you, controlling your reins

What am I?

Thoughts

Two Years Ago To the Day

Two years ago to the day
I looked upon life in a different way
As you listen you may find
How love had forever changed my mind

There was a point in my life
When nobody thought I would find a wife
I thought they were right until that day
Two years ago to the day

Two years ago to the hour
Everything changed from me and mine to us and ours
I knew in that moment I had found
The soul to which my heart would be bound

It felt as if a weight had been lifted
Like time had stopped, reality shifted
Over you my love I wanted to shower
Two years ago to the hour

Two years ago to the very breath
I knew I wanted to be with you, even beyond death
Your heart and mine
In that moment became intertwined

Two hearts became one that Christmas night
And for the first time everything was right
For that moment I was even immune to death
Two years ago to the very breath

Two years ago today
I asked in my own way
If me and mine could be us and ours
And I ask again two years later, to the day, the minute, and hour

Thoughts

Uncertainty

Between two choices I am torn
Deep inside my soul is ripped and worn
For the first time in my life
I am not sure how to deal with my strife

This problem cannot be solved with great ease
It feels like I am hunting for the cure of a disease
For the first time in my mind, body, and soul
All three have their own desires and goals

I have no idea where to go from here
And this uncertainty to my very core sears
Burning with a fury of hate
For not planning every possible fate

I must make a choice
But, this problem is hard to voice
Some might see it as a natural thing
Others would see it makes me less of a human being

But I must make up my own mind
And to my fate, myself I must bind
This binding might send me into oblivion and further
But still I search for the answer with great fervor

It feels as if this holy grail of mine is just out of reach
But I have no-one to ask so they can teach
Teach me where to go, and how to respond
And no locksmith to unlock these bonds

No-one can ever help me come to a conclusion
They would just give me a piece of their delusions
I will be lost until my answer can be found
Then to that fate I will forever be bound

Thoughts

Which are you: Speaking or being spoken of?

By your laughter, I am swallowed
From the inside out my heart is hollowed
I am poison; I am vile
The only bliss I have is denial

This mask of laughter; mask of care
Show my true self I wouldn't dare
Keep pointing; keep laughing—while you can
Keep me exiled—keep me banned

Your laughter fuels my rage
Be gone before I escape my cage
I am the animal of your worst nightmare
Your thoughts and dreams I will ensnare

You glare at me as you hiss
Trust me, you will be first on my list
They are all in for a surprise
Then the questions will arise

It was all in fun—now the fun must cease
My anger is too much—it must be released
Leaving nothing but carnage in my path
You deserve what you get—do the math

To solve the problem—remove the source
You are the center of my discourse
Because of your so-called fun you will die
I listen to you beg—I listen to you cry

How does it feel?
With you gone I will heal
With you gone I will find
My much searched for peace of mind

Think: *Which are you?*

Thoughts

WHY

Have you ever noticed people can't be satisfied?
Needs and desires ever changing, unable to be pacified
Asking for one thing when really wanting another
True desires remaining undercover

Asking for more grass then calling it weeds
Asking for more trees then throwing away the seeds
Saying *shut-up, sit down*, and *go away*
Then they miss you when you're gone for a day

Wanting to be happy; to be at ease
Then avoiding it like a disease
Wanting to be stronger but won't push themselves
Not getting what they want, dreams get shelved

Hidden in the back of their mind, never looking again
Closing the cover before the book's end
The novel that is life, the novel that is love
The great Book of Eternity written by He above

It seems no one wants to find what they are meant to be
So blinded by fear they cannot see
Dreams being beyond the next hill
Having only miles left; quitting even still

Busy trying to lie to the one they cannot deceive
Afraid to run another mile and the reward receive
Instead of chomping at the bit,
They give up, sit down, and quit

Too often to mention, people slow their pace
Instead of staying the course and finishing the race
With the finish line in sight they give in
After quitting everything, what then?

Thoughts

Free of 'Friends'

I am exiled, forced to be alone
Into this solitary life I have grown
They point fingers and force me down
My body walks but I am six feet under ground

They turn their backs on me
They won't let me be free
I walk on egg shells
I walk through a maze of string and tied bells

When I do what they desire
My hate and anger shoot even higher
I am damned if I do, damned if I don't
They tell me not to care—don't worry, I won't

I do what they say
And get shunned anyway
Days I try to fit in, try to talk
They laugh and point and mock

When I am quiet they yell and shout
They try to remove all clout
So be it—I won't conform
I am the wayward soul—see my horns

I will never care—because I cannot win
Push my hate deeper, deeper within
They can only push me so far out the door
Until I fight back—declaring war

No longer trying to please
My pain starts to ease
Now I live for myself—and myself alone
Not bound anymore—no longer a drone

Special Thanks

I would like to thank a whole bunch of people for all of their support and *boots*. There is not enough space to thank everyone for everything, so I will try to thank everyone for something.

First I would like to thank foster care for giving me the ability to see life from as many angles as possible. I would like to thank my "inner demons" for finding my "Outer Angel" for me. Here comes the list: Julie, my Angel. You are the best thing that has ever happened to me. Pops—for being Pops and everything that entails. Mom and Dad—strict, supportive, loving. Ma (Laurie), for realizing it is always worth trying to show how much you care. Jeff for being my first friend and being my best friend to date. Sharon for the hours of conversation about everything and nothing. Linda Kennedy for never giving up on us.

Aaron Tierno—you are missed, thank you for saving my life. Daniel for standing between me and high school bullies. J.D., I mean Garth for showing me it is manly to show love. Uncle Bob for teaching me the game of chess and that it is okay to lose as long as I continue to try. To Russ Jones for being the youngest old guy ever. Kent Jones for keeping everyone young. Kim and Dixon for kicking me in gear. Brian Loza—thanks for being a clown—I tell my friends I know *Iron Man ;)*. Thanks Doc MD, you know for what ;). SSG John S (can't spell your last name to save my life), for being patient in the desert. Phill Cannon for making physics the most fun ever.

Tony and Alice Rodriguez for being champions; I am a better person because I know you. Elder Bigler, Elder Burke, Elder Adams, Elder Cherry, and Sister Smith for bringing love everywhere you go. I know y'all aren't full time mishes anymore, but that is how I will always remember you. Kathy Santos for being the awesomest awesomely patient Submission Representative ever; you are awesome.

Now on to people I don't know but had an influence: Metallica, Rob Zombie, Staind, Drop Kick Murphys, Adema, Dean Martin, Luciano Pavarotti, Reel Big Fish, Mozart, Drowning Pool, Offspring, Disturbed, The Dubliners, Game On. Robin Williams for making humor common place and showing it is okay to be a character (or characters).

Thank you to the USO for keeping soldiers' spirits up since there have been soldiers. THANK YOU TO EVERY SAILOR, SOLDIER, MARINE, and AIRMAN for defending our nation and my rights.

Printed in Great Britain
by Amazon